THE DARK SIDE OF THE CALLING

Pastor Marisol Santos

The Dark Side of the Calling
Copyright © 2024 Pastor Marisol Santos

All rights reserved. No part of this publication may be reproduced, distributed, or transmitted in any form or by any means, including photocopying, recording, or other electronic or mechanical methods, without the prior written permission of the author and publisher, except in the case of brief quotations embodied in critical reviews and certain other noncommercial uses permitted by copyright law.

Scripture quotations marked (NIV) are taken from the Holy Bible, New International Version®, NIV®. Copyright © 1973, 1978, 1984, 2011 by Biblica, Inc.™ Used by permission of Zondervan. All rights reserved worldwide. www.zondervan.com The "NIV" and "New International Version" are trademarks registered in the United States Patent and Trademark Office by Biblica, Inc.™

Translated in English by Manuel Hernandez

Published by: DiViNE Purpose Publishing Co. LLC
www.divinepurposepublishing.com

ISBN: 978-1-948812-38-2

Printed in the United States of America

DEDICATION

To be chosen by God to carry out his will is a great blessing. But it does not exempt us from going through battles, struggles, deserts, trials, and tribulations. In the calling, there are difficult, obscure, and dark moments. My faith is that this book brings peace and strength to your life. I would like to dedicate each experience on these pages to all those who have been separated to do God's will and the reason I am probably still mentally sane.

— *Pastor Marisol Santos*

TABLE OF CONTENTS

Dedication	3
Prologue	7
Introduction	9
Biblical Profiles	13
Loneliness, Depression & Panic Mode	25
Where was God?	37
Conclusion	43
Definitions	46
Bibliography	47
About the Author	49
Notes	51

PROLOGUE

The Dark Side of the Calling
by Manuel Hernandez

It is essentially impossible to determine rules and regulations on how to respond and establish the calling of God in our lives. Jesus himself acknowledged that the kingdom was a daily living of peace, power, justice, and authority in the Spirit. But the Word of God reveals secrets on how to live, recreate, and become assertive of God's calling. When God calls his children, the mandate sets the wheels in motion for a life completely unknown yet set aside for those who willingly respond in the affirmative to God's voice.

The Word of God is a mirror in which the Spirit of God reveals His most intimate secrets. Because of our manmade natural upbringings, understanding the assignment is at first glance at a distance and out of reach. David (Jesse's eighth son) never imagined the journey he was about to embark on when the Prophet Samuel visited his father's house and anointed him as King of Israel.

> "So he asked Jesse, Are these all the sons you have? There is still the youngest, Jesse answered, but he is tending the sheep. Samuel said, Send for him; we will not sit down until he arrives. So he sent and had him brought in. He was ruddy, with a fine appearance and handsome features. Then the LORD said, Rise and anoint him; he is the one. So Samuel took the horn of oil and anointed him in the presence of his brothers, and from that day on the Spirit of the LORD came upon David in power. Samuel then went to Ramah (1 Samuel 16:11-13, New International Version , NIV)."

It was a thirteen-year roller-coaster ride that ended with David's appointment by the elders of Israel as King of God's people. His calling engaged God's purpose with the good, bad, and ugly experiences he would go through because of his decisions during the voyage. *The Dark Side of the Calling* encompasses a unique in-depth look into what happens before, during, and after the calling activates itself and throttles every move we make and every decision we take in the process.

The experience activated a lifetime journey in which David exceeded the boundaries of the expectations of his calling, but the experience/s did not come without growing pains. *The Dark Side of the Calling* is a mirror and a revelation of the journey that men and women embark on when God calls them and sends them on their way to an ongoing journey of discovery and assertion in Jesus Christ.

Joseph (Abraham's great-grandson) was sold and sent as a slave to a foreign land to set the wheels in motion for the largest liberation movement that has ever existed.

> "Then Joseph said to his brothers, I am about to die. But God will surely come to your aid and take you up out of this land to the land he promised on oath to Abraham, Isaac, and Jacob. And Joseph made the sons of Israel swear an oath and said, God will surely come to your aid, and then you must carry my bones up from this place (Genesis 50:24-25, NIV)."

It was a dream that Joseph had and ignorantly voiced to his brothers that almost got him killed but sent him in route toward the fulfillment of his calling.

These up-and-coming pages attempt to display and recreate how some of the men and women that we read in the Bible and history portrayed the calling. The book is a keen revelation of the before, during, and after process of such an experience. Pastor Marisol Santos swiftly captures the struggle, dilemma, and battle of the calling and plants a seed of wisdom in all who have and will be "called" to carry out God's will in ministry leadership. This is a must-read, must-buy, and a wake-up call in times like these.

INTRODUCTION

It was just another day during the week at about 7:00 p.m. The classroom was filled with students waiting for the professor teaching Humanities at Interamerican University, Fajardo Campus. It was the first day of school, and everyone was anxious. They wanted to know who the professor was and the topic he was going to discuss. On the first day, everyone presented themselves. The professor read from the syllabus where he discussed the course, its objectives, and everything related to the activities and assignments required in the class. It was a bit dark, but you could appreciate the beauty of nature, the skies, and green trees through the classroom doors. Suddenly, a tall man with a reddish beard and profound respiration came in walked directly to the board, and wrote with huge letters the following sentence:

> "GOD IS WHO, OF WHOM NOTHING GREATER CAN BE CONCEIVED."

The students were surprised and reflected upon the professor's writing on the board. The professor said: "What do you have to say about the statement?" At first glance, the statement was impactful and many shouted "Wow!" Others expressed their point of view and agreed with such a statement. The professor said, "Today we are going to start to talk about inclusion and deduction. We are going to define inclusion and deduction." During the whole semester, the expression made a huge dent in my heart. Through the years, I analyzed the expression repeatedly. Today, I can say a serious inclusion analysis of the professor's statement had to be made because God is not Whom, God is God, sovereign, eternal, the beginning, and the end. He was not conceived. If it is about the Son of God, humanly speaking, he was born by a woman (but conceived by the Holy Spirit, not by human nature). Then, we would be talking about Emmanuel, who is "God is with us", and we would have to induce completely that truth (Matthew 1:18). God always was, God always is, and God always will be. In Psalms 136, the Psalmist speaks about how God created everything with understanding and science. In the Book of Job from chapters 38 through 41, God speaks to Job from a whirlwind and confronts him with the reality that a lot of times man speaks with words without wisdom. God makes a detailed account of every measure and foundation and with every scientific angle including its geography, cosmos, environment, climate, biology, botany, and astronomy. Furthermore, he explains the earth's brontology, zoology, and the rules he established as Omnipotent over all the creation. Finally, he reiterates the objective of God's existence as the Eternal God, undefeated and unquestionable (Job 40:2). In Psalms 23:4, David expresses his trust in God.

Ever since we are children, in church we are taught the Ten Commandments. Second, to love God above all things. Third, to fear God which is the respect to his creation and all the great things that he has done. As we continue to grow, the Holy Spirit starts to work with our hearts and speaks to us in a variety of ways. Sometimes, he speaks to us through his word. On other occasions, he speaks to us directly to our hearts. On several occasions, the Spirit of God uses people to tell us the truth about his calling and our hearts jump or we are moved when the Spirit uses someone in the prophetic or word of knowledge and tells us what the Lord wants from us.

I remember the experience of a young girl who congregated each Saturday in the home of a missionary. The missionary was part of a Biblical extension class program. She met with a lot of children from the neighborhood and picked them up. She sang, testified, prayed, and gave gifts to the children every Saturday to motivate them to come back the following week. One Saturday while they prayed, God's presence started to manifest itself gloriously. The Lord used the missionary and took her directly to that young girl and the Spirit of God told her "I see a chest, and it is filled with a treasure and gemstones for you." That word stayed engraved in the girl's heart forever.

With her coming of age, the girl saw how God started to work in her life and make her a great preacher and worshipper leading her to the pastorship. On one occasion, a special children and pre-teens service was celebrated. The leader of the celebration invited a pre-teen to preach. When she finished preaching, her mother asked her for participation after she had finished preaching and spoke directly to a rebellious teen who sat in the back part of the church. This young lady lived a hidden sinful life caused by a life filled with hate and abuse from her father. It was revealed through the Spirit of God. When the mother of the preacher called her to come up to the front, she was afraid and thought that God was going to rebuke and punish her. Surprisingly, in a word of wisdom and science, the woman started to describe the great pain that existed in the heart of the tender young girl who was rejected, but God demonstrated the contrary. God spoke words of tenderness and spoke to her about how special she was to God. The young girl fell on her knees crying and receiving consolation from God.

God always speaks to us about our calling. It is exciting to know that he counts on us. He has glorious purposes with all those who put themselves in his hands and submit themselves to God's divine word. Nonetheless, the calling has consequences. In Psalms 23:4, David speaks about valleys of shadow and death, suffering, and a dark side that not everyone is willing to talk about.

This is why in these pages I would like to share the experiences some of these men and women experienced that God utilized powerfully but suffered through extreme circumstances. Although God did not leave them alone, they went through painful processes, weaknesses, and strong temptations. The calling has moments of death and moments of life. There are moments of happiness and moments of sadness. There are moments when we are accompanied; there are also moments of loneliness. There are moments of honor and moments of less honor. Then, there are moments of weakness and moments of strength. There are moments of energy and moments of lack of energy. There are days of encouragement and days of discouragement, but God approved and confirmed the calling. He will sustain it and support it forever.

BIBLICAL PROFILES

Development

The meaning of Psalms is connected primarily with the moving of the fingers—also, a song accompanied by a psalm. *"Psallo"* means to pinpoint or to tear down. Then, to play and sing with a harp and to sing psalms. In Psalms 23, a messianic Psalm, David describes the Lord as a shepherd. David was also describing his own experience because he had been a shepherd in his younger years and caretaker of his father's sheep, Jesse of Bethlehem (1 Samuel 16:10-11). David was the youngest of eight brothers. According to his own experience, I can imagine David with an arp while he relaxed, rested, sang, and composed Psalms to the Lord. However, in verse four of this Psalm, it says: "Yea, though I walk through the valley of the shadow of death, I will fear no evil: for thou art with me; thy rod and thy staff they comfort me."

A valley is usually terrain that is at a lower level than the terrain surrounding it. It is a valley of mountains and hilltops. If you have visited Arizona in the United States, you have been to Moctezuma, a great mountain close to the Huachuca Military Base. If you have been to the top, you are aware that at mountaintop you can appreciate a great and beautiful immense valley. Standing from this view, you can appreciate the grandeur of God's creation. It is super wide and surrounded by mountains; it looks endless.

David had the experience and knew what he was talking about when he mentioned the valley of shadow and death. It is difficult to discern if your enemies are hidden in the mountains or if they are hidden within the terrain. What if they are hidden in the middle of absolute obscurity, without light or a compass, without anything for you to identify them or defend yourself? Additionally, their sole purpose is to harm you, to catch you off guard, and you are not going to be able to see the different types of snakes and ferocious animals waiting to devour you. If there are shadows, everything will look the same, and it will be difficult to differentiate between the images because of the lack of light. Even the clarity of the moon and the stars could provide you with an opaque image of certain things that could make you observe things that are not present. It is like a phantasmagoric image of a dead person, and the valley is immense, and you cannot see with clarity just like what David expresses in Psalms 23:4.

Death is the absence or lack of life. It is the act of killing a person. This originates because of the organic impossibility of sustaining the homeostatic process. It comes from the Latin "mars" or "mortis." Causes of death could be illness, suicide, or some form of trauma. There is natural death produced as a result of pathology or sickness, for example, a cancerous tumor or infectious disease. There is brain death which is characterized by the loss of cognitive and clinical functions of the brain, for example, cephalitis, brain concussion, chronic sepsis, or cranial hemorrhage, amongst others. Finally, sudden death is the one that comes suddenly and unexpectedly, for example, cardiac arrest, or an automobile accident among other processes.

I would like to mention that every man or woman of God in one form or another is called by God and accepts this responsibility and identifies with these processes and similar feelings which I am going to describe in these pages.

Abraham

He was from Ur of the Chaldeans and the son of Terah. He was born around 2166 B.C. in Ur of the Chaldeans. He grew up in a port city to the south of the Persian Gulf. It was a great agricultural center for commercial and manufacturing products. It was also a fertile and rich city. It was about twelve miles from the place believed to be the Garden of Eden. Abraham needed to leave his land and family and march to a land that God would guide him to go to. In Genesis 12:1 the stage was set for Abraham's calling when it states, "The Lord had said to Abram,

'Go from your country, your people and your father's household to the land I will show you.'" (NIV) When he got to Egypt, he said his wife Sarai was his sister because he feared he would be killed. God told him to leave his family, but he brought his nephew Lot with him. Lot followed with all his possessions but had conflicts with his shepherds and because of that, they separated. Lot left and lived in Sodom and Gomorra Valley, and Abraham moved to the land of Canaan. It was difficult for Abraham to believe in God's promises. When God promised him that he would have a son in his old age, his wife suggested he have a child with his servant, and he did not wait and trust the promises God had expressed to him (Genesis 16:3), and this brought him the consequences of having a son, Ishmael, son of his concubine, Hagar. Abraham's decision to have a son brought conflicts between his wife and Hagar, and he had to decide between the promised child (Isaac) and sending Hagar away with her son. This was a very troubling decision for Abraham because he loved his son Ishmael. Abraham tried to solve problems on his own and tried to blame others for his problems. He lied on more than one occasion because he feared for his life and feared losing all the material things that he had. Another difficult moment for Abraham was when God asked him to sacrifice Isaac. After having Isaac in his old age, and his son was coming of age, God tested the faith and loyalty of this man, and he obeyed. Can you imagine this man walking nervously and thoughtfully with many conflicts in his mind as he walked towards the mountain where he was going to sacrifice his son while Isaac asked where the animal for the holocaust was? What a difficult moment for Abraham and Isaac!

Moses

He was from the Levi tribe and Jochebed's son. He became a great leader and Hebrew legislator. When Pharaoh ordered all the Hebrew children to be murdered, his mother hid him for three months in her home, but when she could not hide him no longer, she made a papyrus basket for him and coated it with tar and pitch. Then, she placed the child in it and put it among the reeds along the bank of the Nile. His sister stood at a distance to see what would happen to him. Then

Pharaoh's daughter went down to the Nile to bathe, and her attendants were walking along the riverbank. She saw the basket among the stems and sent her female slave to get it. She opened it and saw the baby. He was crying, and she felt sorry for him. Miriam, Moses' sister intervened and suggested that the princess get a baby sitter to take care of him. The baby sitter was Moses' real mother who took care of him until he was three years old. Moses received the education and wisdom of an Egyptian aristocrat. One day, after Moses had grown up, he went out to where his people were and watched them at their hard labor. He saw an Egyptian beating a Hebrew, one of his people. Looking this way and that and seeing no one, he killed the Egyptian and hid him in the sand. When he was discovered, he ran away.

When God calls him, he tells God that he does not know how to speak (Exodus 4:15). When he fights against the Amalekites, his arms get tired (Exodus 17:12). He worries a lot about the people and hears them from dawn to sunset, trying to be responsible with his work, but it was too much for him (Exodus 18:18). Then, Jethro, gives him administrative recommendations for his benefit and his people. He was in Mount Sinai with God without drinking water or eating and listening to God's voice and his instructions. He prepares and organizes the people according to God's instruction. At a particular moment, he feels emotionally charged, tired, confused, and asked God to take his life (Numbers 11:11-15). He is criticized by his brother Aaron and his sister Miriam (Numbers 12:1). He does not believe God when God tells him to speak to the rock and strikes it twice. He became tired of Israel's complaints (Numbers 20:12). He was not able to enter Canaan because he became rebellious to God's mandate in the Zin desert (Numbers 27:14). He was not able to cross the Jordan; God was angry with him because of the people of Israel. He was only able to see the land from the top of the Pisgah Mountain (Deuteronomy 3:26-27).

Joseph

He was the eleventh son of Jacob and the firstborn of his beloved Rachel. He was born in Padanaram in Mesopotamia. His story is featured in chapters 37-50 in the Book of Genesis. He was envied and belittled by his brothers because his father loved him dearly. For them, he was someone with little or no value who thought was superior to them. It was not like that. Joseph had two dreams that his brothers misinterpreted. One day, his father sent him on a mission to his brothers. When they saw him, they decided to put him in an empty well without feeling pain or having any feelings about Joseph. They sold him as a slave to Ishmaelite merchants. Joseph went to Egypt as a slave and was forgotten by his family. The inexperienced young man became the administrator of Potiphar's household (Pharaoh's captain and official). While he served in Potiphar's house, he was tempted by his wife to sleep with her, but he maintained his integrity and respect for God. As a result, he was imprisoned unjustly. How many fearful nights did this young man live without ever committing one crime? God put him in favor during his time in the prison. In prison, he interpreted two dreams for the Pharaoh's servants. Then, the dreams became real, and those who left the prison because of the interpretation of their dreams forgot about Joseph.

When Pharaoh had a dream that traumatized him, the cupbearer remembered that Joseph interpreted dreams, and Pharaoh sent for him immediately. Joseph interpreted Pharaoh's dream, received favor from God, and was positioned as second in command with authority in the nation of Egypt (Genesis 37-45). God prepared him and positioned him in a place of honor. From a shepherd to a slave to a convicted felon to a governor, Joseph always honored God. At a distance, Joseph continued to miss his father deeply. When famine and hunger filled the land, sure enough, Joseph had a re-encounter with his brothers and his dad. When they met again, his brothers did not recognize him, and in private his heart wept immensely. Finally, he reveals himself to them, forgives them, and takes care of their families and possessions. He feeds them, takes care of them, and protects them, even knowing that they had betrayed him, belittled him, and mistreated him. He lived a large portion of his life without his dad and brothers, but he held no grudges against them. However, he had to go through all that to preserve the life of his family. In life, there are times when you must lose to win, stop growing to grow. We cannot be defeated by the bad things in life; we should use the good to defeat the bad things in life.

Samson

He was born in Zora. He was the son of Manoah of the Dan tribe. He was a Nazareth and dedicated to God from his birth. He could not drink any wine or other fermented drink or eat anything unclean. His head could never be touched by a razor because the boy was to be a Nazarite, dedicated to God from the womb. He would take the lead in delivering Israel from the hands of the Philistines (Judges 16). While he honored God by obeying everything that God had said through the angel, God gave him powerful strength. No animal, enemy, or army could defeat him. Unfortunately, on many occasions, he violated God's orders and laws. His sensuality controlled him. He trusted the wrong people and used his gifts and abilities unwisely. Samson trusted himself and his strength. He fell in love with the wrong woman. When a person falls in love, the heart changes and his or her entire life takes a complete turn. Our feelings are committed, and they dominate us. We are weak considering such a strong feeling. We are ingenuous and allow our feelings to betray us. We are weakened emotionally by that feeling. In Samson's situation, his enemies were trying to find a way to destroy him. Once they accomplished that, they could control and dominate Israel, but he made mistakes and trusted himself and started to judge with sensuality and weaknesses when he fell in love with Delilah. His heart failed him. As a man he fell into a trap that he was not able to get out of. His love and attraction for Delilah were more powerful than his commitment to God. He was not valued as one who was chosen by God even before he was born. His feelings, carnal desires, and passion blinded him and took him to exhaustion. This is when he fell and was tortured, ridiculed, taken as prisoner, and humbled unto God. Finally, he asked God for his strength to take revenge against his enemies: the Philistines. God hears him in his mercy. Samson's mistakes cost him his life. We will never know how many more things God had for him. However, the plan was cut short.

David

The youngest son of Jesse of Bethlehem of Judah and the youngest of eight children. He was a shepherd of his father's sheep. God sent the prophet Samuel to anoint him as the next King of Israel (I Samuel 16:12-13). Because of the king, the people of Israel had chosen, the country was in crisis. The king had been emotionally disturbed when a bad spirit had overtaken him and was jealous of David. One of his first difficult moments was when King Saul started looking at him differently because the women of Israel sang songs after he had defeated Goliath. The women adulated David because he had bravely defeated Goliath (I Samuel 17). Saul was jealous of David because God's presence was with David and the king's daughter Michal loved him. From that moment on, Saul was David's worst enemy and tried to kill him on several occasions (I Samuel 18:28-29). David experienced fear, loneliness, and living far from his family because he had to escape for his life. One time, he acted as a lunatic to live with his enemies in the land of Gat because he feared for his life (I Sam. 21:13-15). Then, when he was established as king in a kingdom of peace, his personal life was intertwined with deep sin when he committed adultery with Bathsheba. Bathsheba, the wife of Uriah, and Hetero one of the soldiers in the army got pregnant from David. David tried to get Uriah to sleep with his wife during one of their stays at home during the war. When he did not sleep with his wife, David ordered a general to put him in the front position of the war to get him killed.

    David abandoned his purpose as king; he was supposed to be in the war. However, he focused on his desires, and he deliberately sinned. Then, he tried to cover his sins and committed premeditated murder. While David was chosen by God to carry out a calling, there could have been different reasons why David fell into such a difficult situation in his relationship with God. He could have been submerged in a comfort zone, maybe he was afflicted, frustrated, and felt betrayed. David's greatness as a leader could have gotten in the way. His thoughtfulness and the negative surroundings are just like what happens to many ministries today. When Nathan the prophet confronted him with God's message, David humbled himself unto God and fasted, prayed, and asked God for mercy recognizing his great wrongdoings and the consequences that he was going to receive as a result of his actions (2 Sam. 11-12).

Elijah

He was called for the ministry during Ahab and Jezebel's time as kings. They called him (Tishbite), and he was from Gilead. He was called when Ahab was under his wife's influence. She became Baals' worshipper of Tyre. He prophesied drought for three years (I Kings 17:1). He was a man of prayer who lived in the caves, or the mountains separated by God. When he prophesied, he did it with the authority and reassurance from God. He was the most well-known and the most dramatic prophet in Israel. God used him in the resurrection of the widow of Zarephath who lived on the Mediterranean coast of Tyre. He also multiplied the oil and the flour for her as well. He was the prophet who represented God in a challenge to the Baal and Asherah priests. Elijah prayed and God responded with fire from the sky demonstrating his power and taking the people to recognize God as the true God, and after that, he killed all the false prophets who prayed to Baal. (I Kings 18).

Under God's authority, Elijah had no fear and was firm and brave, confrontational, decisive, and jealous of God. He knew how to listen to God's voice and transmit God's message to the king, the people, and the Baal prophets. He was not a boring or monotonous prophet. God's hand was with him (I Kings 18:46). After these impressive and powerful things occurred, King Ahab shared these things with his wife, Jezebel. Queen Jezebel sends him a letter and threatens to do the same thing he did to Baal's prophets to him. She has no authority to control God's chosen man. She was furious with Elijah. Then, Elijah decided to leave and save his life thinking that he was more alone than ever. He thought he was the only prophet alive. Elijah the human being was tired of walking through the valley of the shadow of death just like David in Psalms 23:4. He was intensely fatigued and extremely confused. He was weak physically and emotionally, and he asked God to take his life, God sent an angel to wake him up to tell him that there was a long road ahead of him (I Kings 19:5-7). God allowed him to sleep, rest, and eat, but he told him that he needed to get up and move forward. The food strengthened him for forty days and forty nights while he walked to the Horeb mountain, and there he went into the cave with his depression.

This man represented those whom at a particular time were used by God powerfully and were daring to the calling. A person who under the anointing resurrected the dead, healed the sick, did great miracles did everything necessary for God's glory, and received divine revelation. When difficult circumstances such as illnesses, hardships, and burnout start looming on the horizon, questions become the context of the daily interaction with God. When illness and feelings of abandonment overwhelm the person with a calling, confusion, and anxiety come marching into reality. At times, there is even a desire to run and abandon everything. There is an emptiness about the whole experience. You don't feel that God is near or there. The mind starts playing tricks on you. People have a lack of understanding towards this experience and set high expectations on your calling. Others see you as their hero. As a result, we hide in a cave, and we start running without knowing why. This ignites a huge negative influence upon your life, and you feel death is near or the lack of desire to live. It is like having a huge giant in front of you. The giant is affronting you, and you cannot move forward. You try to manage the situation according to your abilities, but it is not enough.

I remember the experience of a woman who was a pastor, and the church of which she was a Pastor was blessed, but the adversary attacked her with all his might. The Pastor felt an enormous desire to get closer to God, and she would lock herself in her room while the Holy Spirit ministered to her daily. On another day, she was locked up in her room while the Holy Spirit ministered to her. However, one day as she walked from the bedroom to the living room to the kitchen, she saw in the Spirit, that a giant and strong being resisted her and bumped into her. She could not affront such a giant because she felt weak and sick. The devil takes advantage of our weaknesses, our feelings, our health conditions, and our fears to limit us and deviate our attention from our calling. He is watching us and following us and in our most vulnerable moments. He attacks us to try and defeat us and stray us away from the pathway. In Elijah's case, the enemy used Jezebel, a diabolical and pagan woman who did not fear God.

Job

The author of the Book of Job is unknown. Some have suggested the names of Moses, Salomon, or Eliud as its author. Its historical timeline puts it between 2000-1800 B.C. The story of Job begins in Uz, probably close to Palestine, between Damascus and the Euphrates River. In the Hebrew Bible, Job is recognized as the first poetic book. For history, it is one of the most ancient books because it alludes to the pyramids (Job 3:14), the plain cities (Job 15:28), and the great flood (Job 22:14). Job was a prosperous man. He had cattle, thousands of sheep, camels, servants, and a big family. He had prestige and was highly favored and recognized. He was a rich man, the richest man among the orientals of his time. He prayed constantly and sacrificed holocausts for the sins of his children. He wanted God to have mercy over them. He was perfect, feared God was righteous, and separated himself from evil (Job 1:1-5). However, in Heaven, God and Satan had a conversation about Job's integrity. The devil accused him of serving God for two reasons: 1. God had given him a lot of riches. 2. God had given him good health. The enemy was sure that if God took away those two things, Job would curse God (Job 1:9-11). God authorized the devil to touch him, but God did not give him authority over his life. From this moment on, Job's life started to experience some terrible trials and tribulations. As a result, Job started experiencing the valley of shadow and death that David mentioned in Psalms 23:4. His first trial was when the Sabeans took all his cattle and killed all his servants who worked the land. Second, he lost his sheep, and the shepherds were destroyed by fire. Third, a Chaldean squadron stole his camels and killed the servants. Fourth, his children died when a strong wind destroyed the house where they were in. Finally, Job falls victim to a terrible illness considered nauseous and painful during his time. It could have been the Hansen illness caused by a *Mycobacterium leprae*. According to the Centers for Disease Control and Prevention, "The disease affects the nerves, skin, eyes, and lining of the nose. The bacteria attack the nerves, which can become swollen. This can cause the affected areas to lose the ability to sense touch and pain, which can lead to injuries, like cuts and burns. If left untreated, the nerve damage can result in paralysis of hands and feet."

This man lost everything, including his family, a valley, and the shadow of death as David expressed in Psalms 23:4. Then, his wife tells him to curse God and die. She lost her trust, the love and care for Job, and the fear of God. Instead of support, his friends came by and accused his integrity and character. Job's body was rotten. Ultimately, he was all alone, abandoned, sick, sad, reproached, rejected, isolated, and separated from society like a homeless person without value to society. A man of the people and for the people abandoned by a society that he helped in so many ways.

At times, we don't understand why things happen the way they happen. Furthermore, we don't understand what the objective is and/or purpose. Job wanted to find out the answers to so many questions. He wanted to know God. He was so frustrated at one point that he did not want to be born and wished he was dead. He lost hope and yet he trusted in God (Job 3:3-11).

Jeremiah

The date of his ministry was during 627-586 B.C., and his message was targeted to Judah. The prophet grew up in the priestly city of Anathoth. He was the son of Hilkiah the priest, and the Lord separated him before he was born. He was not allowed to marry or have children, and God used him in prophecy to warn the people and kings about their sins. He also warned them of the punishment that awaited them, to which he received severe opposition, persecution, discouragement, humiliation, scourging, imprisonment, tension, pain, and loneliness (Jeremiah 1). The Lord gave him the power to uproot and destroy, to ruin and tear down, but also to build and plant. His first opponents were the men of Anathoth, his hometown city. They threatened to kill him. He was humiliated by the priests and leaders. He was beaten, put in the stocks, a wooden and iron trap that was used to trap animals where they remained motionless, a type of humiliating punishment where they left him almost naked, motionless, sunbathing, and serene, cold, and hot while people passed by, looked at him and ridiculed him (Jeremiah 20). Then under the reign of

Zedekiah, while Jeremiah was a prisoner, his enemies demanded his death by putting him in a filthy cistern, which was already a muddy dungeon, and there he sank into the mire. (Jeremiah 38:6), but he was rescued by an Ethiopian who had compassion for the prophet's charisma. (Jeremiah 38:7-13).

Jeremiah was spiritually mature and very brave. He was dedicated completely to God and to what God had commanded him to do. Despite a difficult prophetic message, in his intimate moments, he cried for the people. At different times, he went through a terrible depression, and he expressed feeling ridiculed and mocked by so many that he even cursed the day he was born. The day his mother gave birth to the prophet she did not want him to be blessed. The man who told his father that a boy had been born to him, said "Because he did not kill me in the womb." He had no wife to comfort him or encourage him or talk to him, no children to enjoy himself with or give him any kind of encouragement. He felt weak, lonely, disappointed, and defeated, that is, in his humanity he despaired, he became sad, and in his thoughts, he practically gave up. In his internal emotions, he exploded, and he became vulnerable and sensible like the others; this is when he walks through the valley of shadow and death that David mentions in Psalms 23:4.

In the calling, there are many situations and processes. We have seen this in the stories of the men I have described here. There are stages I am going to describe hitherto.

LONELINESS, DEPRESSION & PANIC MODE

It is called chronic loneliness when there are feelings of social isolation. Consequently, these moments are extended and are characterized by a continued and constant desire to isolate oneself from those who surround you. Additionally, the inability to connect with others may provoke insecurity, low self-esteem, and anxiety. According to the *Real Academia Española,* this is defined as the voluntary lack of or involuntary lack of company, a negative mood or melancholy that is felt as the result of the absence, death, or loss of someone or something. It is the desire of not wanting to connect with anyone or anything. It is also the desire to live alone or to live life alone because you have felt betrayed by someone and the desire to thrive and struggle disappears. However, distancing from a place of loneliness may cause changes that may end up affecting you and ultimately send you into an abyss of sadness, abandonment, and spirituality that every human being experiences every day. According to the Centers for the Disease (CDC), "Loneliness and social isolation are a risk of public health for older adults that affects a significant number of people in the United States and puts them at risk of falling into dementia and other difficult illnesses. A new report from the Academy of Science, Engineering, and Medicine (NASEM) indicates that a third of adults who are forty-five years of age or more feel lonely, and one-fourth of those sixty-five or more are socially isolated.

Older adults are at greater risk of social isolation because it is more probable that they encounter other situations like living alone, losing relatives and friends, having chronic illnesses, and loss of auditory senses.

Loneliness: Risks for Health

Although it is difficult to measure social isolation and loneliness specifically, there is strong evidence that sustains that many adults ages fifty and older are socially isolated or lonely in ways that put their health at risk. Recent studies found the following:

- Social isolation increases the risk of a person passing away prematurely for all the ill-related reasons. The risks are as significant as death because of smoking, obesity, or physical inactivity.
- Social isolation is associated with a 50% of the risk of contracting dementia.
- Poor social relationships (characterized by social isolation or loneliness) were associated with a 29% increased risk of heart disease and a 32% increased risk of stroke.
- Loneliness is associated with greater risks of depression, anxiety, and suicide.
- Loneliness in patients with cardiac diseases is associated four times more an increase of 68% in hospitalization to an increase of 57% in the risk to the emergency room.

According to the newspaper, "EL PAIS", a global newspaper in Spain, in its Health and Well-Being section and published on January 10th, 2023, by Jessica Mouzo, loneliness, and social isolation are considered a global and public health crisis, and for many experts "an epidemic", although its real dimension is immeasurable.

A document published in 2021 by the World Health Organization (OMS) states that between 20% and 34% of older persons in China, Europe, Latin America, and the United States feel lonely. Additional published research recently in the *British Medical Journal* found that despite a considerable lack of data, a variable prevalent in different world regions and different ages of adolescents varied by 9.2%, in Southeast Asia by 14.4% in the Western Mediterranean in European adults; the lowest levels prevailed in the North (from 3% in young adults to 5.2% in older adults) and the highest levels are in Eastern Europe (7.5% in the younger and 21% and higher in the elderly).

Loneliness is part of the valley of the shadow and death that Godly men and women go through within their ministry, but as David said in Psalms 23:4: "I will fear no evil"

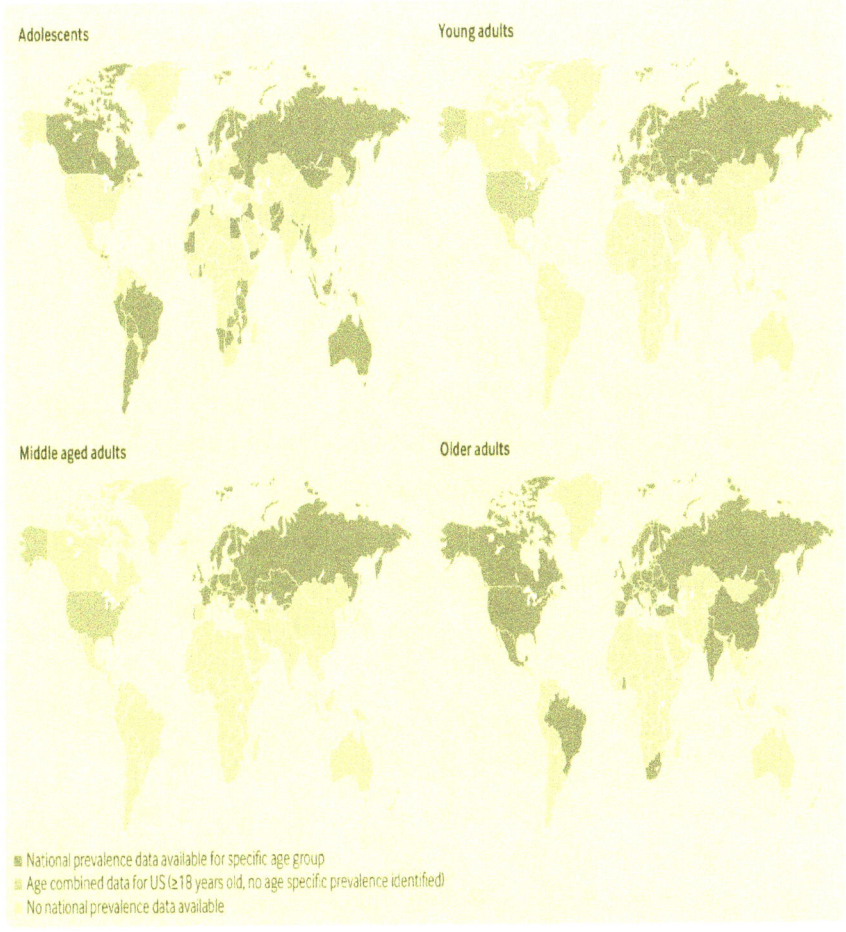

Depression

According to Dr. Craig Sawchuk, a clinical psychologist from the Mayo Clinic, depression is the emotional trauma that causes an extreme and constant sadness feeling and a lack of interest in doing different activities. Also known as "major depressive trauma" or "clinical depression." It affects the feelings, thoughts, and behavior of a person. It may cause a variety of physical and emotional problems. It is possible that you have difficulties doing daily routine activities, and that at times you feel that life is not worth living.

Symptoms:

- Feelings of sadness, desire to cry, an emptiness or hopelessness
- Anger issues, short-temperedness, or frustration, and in many cases for unimportant things
- Lack of interest or pleasure in many of the daily activities or all activities, like sexual relationships, hobbies, and sports
- Modifications in sleep, like insomnia or excessive sleeping. Some people spend days in their rooms without wanting or desiring to leave
- Feeling tired and lack of energy, even for simple and small tasks that require a bit more effort
- Lack of appetite, weight loss, more food cravings, and obesity
- Anxiety, agitation, or unsettledness
- Slowness to reason, difficulties in making simple reasonings. Consequently, the mind becomes lazy
- Feelings of worthlessness or guilt, fixation on past failures, or self-reproach
- Difficulty thinking, concentrating, making decisions, and remembering things, affecting work and productivity
- Frequent or recurring thoughts about death, suicidal thoughts, suicide attempts, or suicide
- Inexplicable physical problems, like headaches, back pain, shoulder pain, or headaches

The World Health Organization or WHO wrote the following information on September 13, 2021:

Facts & Figures

- Depression is a common mental disorder. Worldwide, an estimated 5% of adults suffer from depression.
- Depression is the world's leading cause of disability and is a major contributor to the overall global burden of disease.
- Depression affects women more than men.
- Depression can lead to suicide.
- There are effective treatments for depression, whether mild, moderate, or severe.

Depression can come into the lives of anyone, celebrities or simple people, professionals or untrained people, leaders of nations or armies, pastors, and servants of God in general. How many soldiers, after finishing their training or leaving the war, fall into a terrible depressive condition that has led them to have an extreme dependence on narcotics or the use of alcohol to abandon themselves or distance themselves from society and their families? How many people who were once productive people and bulwarks are today homeless or in the mountains as wanderers because at a given moment, they did not know how to handle the dark moments that came into their lives? They did not know how to face them.

Many ministers have not been able to prepare for their retirement from the ministry. They do not know how to plan and have found themselves in a condition of despair, depression, and sadness without knowing what else to do after they leave some great ministerial position. Others, however, even if they are already tired and exhausted, no longer feel God's calling. It is even more shocking when we read news of pastors who, because of the depression in which they had been immersed for a long time, committed suicide, leaving a beautiful congregation or a fruitful ministry. Perhaps, because they did not have the right support, because of the pressure and demand of the ministry, or because they did not know how to balance the calling with their personal and family lives. It is not only the spiritual area that needs help, but also the emotional, economic, family, sexual, and psychological areas, but many organizations limit themselves to offering these types of services to their workers. Unfortunately, the so-called men and women who are passionate about God's work and strive for it, do not dare, or have the confidence to talk about their weaknesses or struggles for fear of being judged or punished. On the other hand, we are faced with ministerial pride or the fact that they know that they are not well or in an emergency and they do not seek help, they do not confess their fears or mental battles.

On the American television program Daystar on February 16, 2023, on the program, the American ministers David and Pamela Mann testified how he being a man of God went through depression and recognized this and sought help because he felt like he was in a dark room, slowly dying in a corner not knowing what he could do, but he asked for help and said to himself, what can I do. The story goes that he prayed and prayed until his knees hurt, but he knew that something else was missing. He did not miss any services, and he did his part, but he felt a great battle inside him. When David says in Psalm 23:4, "Though I walk in a valley of shadow and death, I will fear no evil," it was because he had already experienced it in his flesh, all those feelings that bring loneliness, depression, panic, threat, and so many more. The great men of the Bible experienced these symptoms repeatedly. I will be talking to you about three symptoms that attack ministers and ministries alike. At the same time, the consequences are loneliness, depression, and panic attacks. I have some evidence that confirms what I am talking about.

News Clips of Pastors affected by Trauma, Mental Illness and Depression:

Los Angeles Times:

"A young pastor preached about depression, then killed himself. His widow wants to help others by talking about it." Article written by Hailey Branson Potts on December 23, 2018

The Washington Post:

Jimmy Swaggart and the Snare of Sin: *"A Saga of Obsession and Anguish, Played out on a Bayou Highway"* Article written by Art Harris

Los Angeles Times:

Pastor and Mental Health Advocate Jarrid Wilson Dies by Suicide Before his death, he tweeted, *"Loving Jesus doesn't always cure suicidal thoughts."* Article written by Roxanne Stone, Emily McFarland Miller, Alejandra Molina on September 10, 2019

Panic Attacks

According to the U.S. National Library of Medicine (Medlineplus.gov), a panic attack is a sudden feeling of terror without apparent danger. It is a type of anxiety disorder where the person feels that they are losing control and even affects their physical condition by giving the following signs:

- Rapid heartbeat (tachycardia)
- Chest or stomach pain
- Shortness of breath
- Weakness or dizziness
- Perspiration
- Heat or chills
- Tingling or numbness

Once upon a time, there was a person who started working a night shift with more responsibilities and new things to learn. She had people living in her house that were helping her to pay for the utilities. Although they were adults, she felt responsible for them. In church, she had responsibilities, and she had to make plans, preach, teach, educate, and do other tasks as well, but one day she had an accident that immobilized her for some time. She started going through a legal process, and the medications that she took started giving her secondary effects which she was not accustomed to. As a result, there were strong legal and medical decisions that she needed to make. According to her doctor and lawyer, she was told that she was under stress and pressure, and this was not going to let her heal. She was told that she needed to decide for her health and well-being.

She began to feel rejected, lonely, disconnected, distraught and her chest tightened. She could not sleep well, and her conscience did not stop oppressing her as she was not fully sure of the decisions she had to make because this was going to cost her something that she loved very much; her ministry, her work, the people close to her. The people closest to her began to move away during her condition. She cried about everything, and she was very sensitive to almost everything.

She experienced discouragement, opposition, indecisions more than ever, confusion, distrust, and laziness. Then, she remembered that in the middle of everything, and in one instance she ran out crying from her room in desperation without hardly being able to breathe with a tight chest. At the same time, someone hugged her and what was oppressing her started to let go of her. Subsequently, she experienced a panic attack, but the most terrible thing was that she was living in sin, and that was deteriorating her relationship with God and her spiritual growth. Finally, she decided to confess her sins, renew her relationship with Christ, and put her life back on track.

The value of the ministry is greater than the trials and tribulations of the ministry. We cannot love the ministry more than God. We cannot change the love for Christ for another type of love. The relationship with Jesus is above and beyond any other relationship. Positions, appointments, recognitions, medals, trophies, or fame cannot and will not fulfill the necessity of the presence of the Holy Spirit in the soul and our hearts. Like Zuleyka Barreto states in her hymn "We can lack everything but his presence, let them all leave but not the Holy Spirit" …. She learned that in life it is better to lose than to win. Today, you give but tomorrow you receive. And that sometimes in our lives and in a moment, everything seems dark. Then, God's presence in a new day arrives to give you hope and light on the horizon. Consequently, you learn that your calling is not yours, and it belongs to God.

God cannot do what he can do where there is sin. There is a call to stop and sit down on a rock on the road to rest and recuperate strength. At first, it may seem things are unjust, but the Holy Spirit starts to delineate things accordingly. The Spirit of God has a way of fixing things that are unresolved or on hold. At the same time, he allows us to see his glorious acts and salvation. We cannot continue to drag things from the past. Although we may think that we are doing a lot of good, we are digging a great hole that sidetracks our blessings. As a result, we can see how much mercy, forgiveness, and love, our Savior has extended to us. God's everlasting peace is worth more than a thousand worlds like this one. The holiness of Christ is more desirable than a direct deposit. It is better to be rejected here on earth than in heaven.

> **Jeremiah 6:16:** "Thus saith the Lord, stand ye in the ways, and see, and ask for the old paths, where is a good way and walk therein, and ye shall find rest for your souls. But they said, We will not walk therein."
>
> **Proverbs 28:13:** "Whoever conceals his transgressions will not prosper, but he who confesses and forsakes them will obtain mercy. Whoever conceals their sins does not prosper, but the one who confesses and renounces them finds mercy."
>
> **Romans 12:21:** "Do not be overcome by evil but overcome evil with good."

In the television program *Ministry Now* on the *Daystar Television Network* Pastor Jimmy Rollins spoke about the experience of meeting his wife and immediately saying: she will be my wife. They got married and had some weeks of happiness until the first conflicts in their marriage flourished. Pastor Rollins tells us how the ministry grew, but there was no communication at home. His wife started drinking, eating, and working excessively, but they knew that things were not right. They loved each other, but there was no understanding of their roles. Each one had a particular point of view, and both thought they were right about things. Their family was affected because of their differences and attitudes towards each other. Both were making incorrect decisions and walking in opposite directions. They were trying to escape from the situation, but it was very difficult for them to do so. For his wife, it was normal to drink alcohol because where she was born and grew up (Switzerland) people drank alcohol from an early age. She started drinking alcohol when she was ten years old.

This couple started going through the valley of shadow and death (Psalms 23:4) in their marriage, in the family, and in the ministry. After these things happened, divorce became a topic of conversation until they found counseling, and they fought for their marriage, family, and ministry until they fixed the areas in their life that needed support. They also allowed the Lord and his divine word to change their hearts and the way they treated each other. This man changed his prayer and intentionally focused it on his family. Consequently, God started sharing his divine grace in their lives.

I share this news report from Humberto Casanova in News from the United Methodist Churches Council, *"Illnesses That Infect The Whole Congregation."* This was written by Owen, Pastor of the First Methodist Church of Chanute Kansas.

Ten Things that Kill the Ministry

1. When the church has a deeply rooted habit and the church is not open to a change for its well-being.

2. When there are pessimistic people who only complain and accuse and don't look for a solution.

3. Obsessive and fearful people who like to control everything and desperately seek to be the center of attention.

4. People who are always trying to limit the growth of the ministry because of the lack of a solid budget.

5. Those who think that their group is right and have no vision for growth to receive everyone for Christ.

6. Members who have not been able to develop the ability to think for themselves and hide behind others.

7. People who prefer to stay comfortable and do not take risks.

8. People who react but do not act unto situations and challenges.

9. Those who are not capable of dreaming or let the Pastor dream by himself. When a church does not dream, it cannot survive or grow.

10. We should all preach and evangelize others: it is not only the responsibility of the leader alone.

WHERE WAS GOD?

Biblical and secular men and women who have been through difficult circumstances in the middle of their calling have experienced the dark side of the experience. Just like David experienced it (Psalms 23:4), not counting the thousands and thousands of men and women who continue to go through difficulties, tribulations, anguish, and persecutions, and who are in the middle of battle or struggling in bellicose situations. "Do not fear because you will be with me." (Psalms 23:4)

We could ask ourselves where God was. In the middle of each stage and trial, where was God? Maybe none of God's servants thought that God had already separated them for his purpose or in favor of his people and the Gospel.

It is a great divine honor to be separated and chosen by the Sovereign God. The Supreme God chose weak, dreadful, and estranged men and women (I Cor. 1:27-31), to embarrass the wise and so-called powerful of the world. He put his treasure in cups of clay. We are his children living in this body made of dust and bones, fragile to temperature, cold and heat, to the tempests and tornados, to the cyclones and winter, to fire and water, to the wind and desert to dangerous animals like our own species, limited to space and time. So that the excellence of his power comes from God and not us (2 Cor. 4:7-9).

He promised Abraham a great nation. Then, he protects him when he relocates to Egypt and deceives Pharaoh and an entire nation saying that his wife Sarai was his sister. He did not allow the death of his nephew and sent angels to take care of him and defend him. The angels guided him out of Sodom and Gomorra. (Gen. 12-13). God promised to bless him, and he fulfilled his promise. In Abraham's old age, he gave him his son, Isaac. Although he proved Abraham's obedience, changed his name while keeping his son alive, and gave him a wife. God was always taking care of Abraham, his possessions, and his family.

When David was insignificant, ignored even by the prophet Samuel. The Omnipresent chose and anointed him to be the second King of Israel. He stands him up against Goliath, the Philistines, King Saul, the people, and his brothers and gives him victory in that war that Israel was already losing. He honors him in front of the people of Israel. As his calling grows, God protects him from the same King who had sent him to battle the Giant. After he sits on the throne, God grants him peace, honor, and blessings. During his reign, David sinned against God. And God ultimately kept his promises to David.

The Bible says that Elijah was a man subject to human passions, but God gave him victory in his battles because of his fervent prayers in every prophecy and in every event that Elijah was used by God. Because he sought God's presence, God supported him. When he called upon God, the Lord came to the rescue of his son. When he went through that terrible depression, God never abandoned him. Then, he woke him up, fed him, and let him rest to recuperate strength. Human beings feel exhausted and frustrated. When he thought he was alone, God told him that he was not alone. He also stressed that others had not given up and surrendered to the opposition. God encouraged him to move forward, to wake up to obtain more victories. In a final show of victory, God elevated him to the heavens in a chariot in front of his disciple Elisha.

Job was one of the men who went through a very difficult process. Some will say that without reason because he was a man of integrity. It was because God wanted him to go through that. Despite the anguish, suffering, and pain, God provided him with strength and victory. God without us continues to be God, but without him we are nothing. Job went through a terrible experience, but it reaffirmed him more in his intimate relationship with God. According to his own words, he had heard about God, but this tragic and heartfelt experience provided him with the ability to know and see God firsthand. God blessed him even more than the first time. Job was an example of being loyal to God with everything or nothing.

If you were to ask me what I want at this stage of my life, I would say to share my life and my dreams with that person who has not yet come into my life. I want to travel, enjoy, go to different places and get to know the relics of the oldest stories in the world, go to countries that I have never been to like Israel, Spain, Rome, Switzerland, England, Greece, Germany, Japan, and many other places, continue studying for my doctorate, teach all that God has allowed me to learn, write my book "Inequalities of Life", to re-record the Glory of the Lord and how it has inspired me and then transition when the Lord wants me to die in peace. It did not happen to Jeremiah like that, but from before he was born, he was separated by God to bring a word of rebuke and warning. Although it was hard and strong for him and very sad, the Lord always gave him strength and comforted him every time he cried again and again, because God knew how strong it was for him as a young man and as a man to feel often alone.

Each word that the Lord put in his mouth; God supported him. He was not embarrassed. God honored his ministry. Jeremiah honored God as well; he never said anything that did not come from God. Although Jeremiah did not live in his birthplace in his latter days, he lived in peace. God put him in a position of authority where people respected him.

I am sure that before the ministers featured here went through anguish or difficult processes that they went through, God surely revealed himself to them and warned them. God always prepares us.

It is not God's will to leave any of his children in dishonor. He does not want his children to go through unwarranted or embarrassing situations. God does not like to play with his servants. Subsequently, he does not allow his servants to play with his purposes. God's purposes are serious and plentiful. There is pressure in the calling. Without a doubt, there are physical, psychological, financial, and family pressures in the calling. The commitment to God's calling requires a deep and profound dedication to his vision and understanding. This is a process. To top all that, there is a spiritual battle which is the strongest of all. The war against the devil and the flesh is the worst of all. Our three enemies are the world, the devil, and the flesh, but the worst of the three is the flesh.

Christ said in John 16:33 "I have told you these things, so that in me you may have peace. In this world, you will have trouble. But take heart! I have overcome the world." He left us the reassurance of peace because he knew through personal experience that there would be much affliction. He was victorious and because he was victorious, we are more than victorious (Rom. 8:37). In terms of the devil in James 4:7: "Submit yourselves, then, to God. Resist the devil, and he will flee from you." If we live a dedicated and active life in prayer, fasting, and obedience to the Word, the devil will have to flee. Christ was tempted by the devil before he began his ministry but in his third temptation, Jesus said to him, "Away from me, Satan! For it is written: Worship the Lord your God and serve him only." (Matthew 4:10)

However, the flesh is weak and our worst enemy lives in us for 24 hours a day, 365 days a year. It does not matter how many fasting days and how many hours you have prayed; the flesh always haunts us with its passions and sinful desires against pleasing God. It is not interested in desires that please God according to his perfect and holy will but against God's perfect purposes. The Bible says in Galatians 5:17-22 "For the flesh desires what is contrary to the Spirit, and the Spirit what is contrary to the flesh. They conflict with each other so that you are not to do whatever you want. But if you are led by the Spirit, you are not under the law. The acts of the flesh are obvious: sexual immorality, impurity, and debauchery; idolatry and witchcraft; hatred, discord, jealousy, fits of rage, selfish ambition, dissensions, factions, and envy; drunkenness, orgies, and the like. I warn you, as I did before, that those who live like this will not inherit the kingdom of God. But the fruit of the Spirit is love, joy, peace, forbearance, kindness, goodness, faithfulness, gentleness, and self-control. Against such things, there is no law. Those who belong to Christ Jesus have crucified the flesh with its passions and desires."

The reality is that momentarily sin feels satisfying, but its consequences are deadly. Romans 8:6 states: "The mind governed by the flesh is death, but the mind governed by the Spirit is life and peace." John 6:63 states: "The Spirit gives life; the flesh counts for nothing. The words I have spoken to you—they are full of the Spirit and life." 1st John

2:1 state: "My little children, these things write I unto you, that ye sin not. And if any man sin, we have an advocate with the Father, Jesus Christ the righteous." Whom better than our Savior who knows what each one of us struggles in his mind and flesh. In Hebrews 2:18 states "Because he suffered when he was tempted, he can help those who are being tempted." We will not fear because he is with us. God will never abandon us as orphans without a father. Furthermore, he does not disarm a soldier to arm another because he has his armaments that are more than enough for the entire army.

Also, he does not send anyone out to war without training. Even as such, God accompanies you into the battlefield. When we are tempted, it is not God who tempts us because he does not tempt anyone. We are tempted through our concupiscence and carnal desires, and our pride. Consequently, the devil takes occasion and tempts us.

God comes to our rescue, and showers us with courage and authority, gives us understanding and wisdom, speaks to us, and shares his revelation with us. In addition, he shows us and gives us vision even during the valley of shadow and death. Without Him we can do nothing, we will not win the war. Nothing is impossible with God. He has all the power to break and build, to tear down and raise again, to humble and exalt, to curse and bless. He is not a God made of wood, he is not the work of hands that have mouths but do not speak, ears but do not hear, noses but do not smell, hands but do not feel, feet but do not walk, they do not speak with their throats, our God is in heaven (Psalms 115).

Truthfully, and with a wrong sense of justice, man takes justice in his hands and revenge takes control of the situation. Mercy and compassion are completely lost in translation. Even discipline and self-control are forgotten in the desire to get back or force a personal hand on someone. Looking the other way and devaluating others as things or people of little or less value, believing themselves to be superior, but we must look to Christ and focus on our goal. Yes, it is the prize of the supreme calling of God in Christ Jesus. We were gifted with lifting, restoring, and forgiving one another. Always trusting that He is with us, as Jeremiah said in chapter 20:11, "But the Lord is with me like a mighty giant…"

CONCLUSION

The rod in Hebrew means Shebet. The shepherds use the Shebet to easily count the sheep. It is a symbol of power and authority. During ancient times, the rod was a wooden club finished at the top with a ball in which strong spikes were embedded. The shepherds knew how to manipulate this rod as a weapon of defense with astonishing skill, and with it, they drove away wild beasts and protected the flock. In this way, the sheep learned not to fear any evil, trusting in the ability and protection of their shepherd. Silence also allowed them to pull the sheep by the middle of their bodies when they strayed and return them to safety and security.

In the beginning, God's correction is painful but, in the end, it brings peace and security. Discipline and correction at the right time restore and heal. That is why the psalmist expressed that they brought breath into his life. It is filling yourself with a feeling or a quality that God wanted in the life of the psalmist. On many occasions, we lose focus and vision, and we lose sight of the main objective, perhaps because the compass is dirty or without batteries, or it may be due to a lack of new ideas or motivation, due to the extreme exhaustion that comes to us many times, or the lack of motivation of those who are supposed to be by our side to help us and are more unfocused than ourselves.

In other moments, our Faith and trust lessen, and our vision is blinded, shuts down the oil or the flame that was there at the beginning. Fatigue, lack of rest, and the many responsibilities give way to the feeling that we are not enough. Consequently, it brings carelessness, lack of self-confidence, and despair. Once you make fast-paced and wrong decisions without prayer and meditation, it is like watching a volcano erupt that is about ready to explode, hot to its maximum capacity, spreading lava everywhere but without fully knowing what is happening inside. It is not until it erupts and explodes that all the lava comes out burning, and the fire burns and destroys everything in its course. God demonstrates his love with correction on time. He speaks to us with sweet words. Parallel to his sweetness is his whip. God also punishes us. Yet his love and tenderness endure and outweigh the punishment. That part of God expresses his mercy and how compassionate he is. God's forgiveness leaves us naked, and it allows us to see how fragile and deficient we are. This is when we have a rude awakening and wake up to a great reality. We are nothing without God and without him, we cannot do anything. Because he loves us, he corrects us, punishes us, warns us, and alerts us.

One who is called by God is not exempt from passing through the valley of shadow and death, nor from feeling lonely or sad, abandoned or frustrated. We are easy targets for the enemy of our souls all the time, in the day or night, morning and afternoon, in cold weather, or hot weather, in winter or summer. It does not matter how much professional preparation or how naïve you are, whether you are rich or poor, guile or simple, strong or weak, as long as we are in this body full of weaknesses and committed, we will be in a relentless war. May God shelter us under his wings to protect us from all evil, to raise the fallen, and to restore the helpless and needy. May God's love always be sheltering us day by day and may the blood of Jesus cover us. Let his rod rebuke our adversary as often as possible. May God's love always cover us daily. Let his rod rebuke us accordingly. May he pull us to him when we are going astray to save and free ourselves from the chains of disaster and destruction. May he also straighten us out and heal us from the wounds that this call leaves us which at the same time is an honor.

May the Lord grant the church power of restoration and may the church continue to do its work of praying, seeking him in Spirit and truth, and fasting for one another. That it may always continue to form women and men willing to do the will of God. May his children become his watchmen and voice of warning in these challenging times, and that we continue to live until the Father decides. These are times of constant changes where Biblical values and important principles of life are in complete disarray. The church must take advantage of the opportunities to build schools and academies. The church must continue to serve food and provide shelter and clothing to the downtrodden, homeless, and impoverished. The church must continue to create new music programs, universities, etc. The church must continue to form good leaders, pastors, evangelists, deacons, bishops, and leaders who are committed to the Word of God and who can provide a good example and continue to proclaim the good news of salvation to the entire world. Christian organizations, ministries, and denominations must offer support in all types of counseling for ministers in a personal, confidential, and professional manner in times of crisis.

May men and women of God continue to rise who are not ashamed of this powerful gospel everywhere. Today, God is active in men and women in government. There are congressmen, senators, lawyers, doctors, teachers, professors, soldiers, merchants, instructors, directors, bankers, and policemen, who will raise the banner of this precious gospel of Jesus Christ.

The church has psychologists and therapists who are willing to help and support the body of Christ in its moments of crisis (like the ministry of Pastor Keila Angulo in Puerto Rico with Free Family Therapy, a place that provides free therapy for families, groups, or individuals. KZ).

Not to be left to die alienating, marginalizing, or rejecting them for this or that. That the barriers of division and disunity among the church be broken.

On one occasion someone said that the only army that abandons its soldiers is the church. And this is seen when someone who at one time was an instrument used mightily in Christ, falls from grace, but what do the people do about it? Many times, they forget them, condemn them, belittle them, and treat them badly, but what would Jesus do in your place? It is more than proven in the Bible that the child whom God loves, disciplines with timely correction, heals, and restores (Heb. 12:6-7). We must seek help when we need it, not reach a position where it is already too late. Do not be afraid, God will be with us and encourage us.

DEFINITIONS

1. **Science** - It is the certain knowledge of things.

2. **Geography** - Geography is the science that studies the Earth and its characteristics, as well as the living beings that inhabit it.

3. **Cosmos** - (From the Greek: "kosmos" – world.) means a system of the world, or the Universe as an integral whole subject to the laws of motion of matter.

4. **Environment** - A set of circumstances or conditions external to a living being that influence its development and activities.

5. **Climatology** - Climatology studies long-term variations in the weather.

6. **Biology** - science that deals with living beings considering their structure, functioning, evolution, distribution, and relationships.

7. **Botany** - Botany is that branch of Biology that deals with the integral study of plants, their description, classification, distribution, and relationships with other living beings.

8. **Astronomy** - is the science dedicated to the investigation of everything related to the stars such as planets, comets, satellites, meteorites, stellar and interstellar bodies, motions, and principles.

9. **Brontology** - Brontology is the part of meteorology that studies storms and everything related to them. It comes from the Greek words bronté - thunder and logos - science.

10. **Zoology** - Zoology is a word that comes etymologically from the Greek *zoos* (animal) and *logos* (science or treatise), so zoology can be considered the science of animals.

BIBLIOGRAPHY

Books:

1. Comentario Bíblico. *Isaías*. (1983). El Paso, Texas. Editorial Mundo Hispano.
2. Grupo Nelson. (1960). *Biblia del Diario Vivir: Versión Reina Valera*. Carol Stream, IL. Caribe.
3. Vila, Escuain. (1985) *Nuevo Diccionario Bíblico Ilustrado*. Barcelona, España. CLIE
4. Vine, W.E. (1999). *Diccionario Expositivo de Palabras del Antiguo y del Nuevo Testamento Exhaustivo*. Nashville, TN. Caribe
5. Willmington, Harold L. (1995). *Auxiliar Bíblico Portavoz*. Gran Rapids, Michigan. Editorial Portavoz.
6. Wood, Leon J. (1983). *Los Profetas de Israel*. Gran Rapids, Michigan. Editorial Portavoz.

Internet:

7. *10 cosas que matan el ministerio*. United Methodist News Service. (2013, February 6). https://www.umnews.org/es/news/10-cosas-que-matan-el-ministerio
8. Branson-Potts, H. (2019, September 13). *Otro joven pastor que abogaba por la salud mental muere por Suicidio*. Otro joven pastor que abogaba por la salud mental muere por suicidio. https://www.latimes.com/espanol/https:/www.latimes.com/california/articulo/2019-09-12/california-mega-iglesia-pastor-suicidio-sanidad-mental
9. Centers for Disease Control and Prevention. (2021). *Soledad y Aislamiento Social Vinculados a afecciones graves*. Centers for

Disease Control and Prevention. https://www.cdc.gov/aging/spanish/features/lonely-older-adults.html

10. Mouzo, J. (2023, January 11). *La Soledad, UN Problema de Salud Pública Que Aumenta el Riesgo de enfermar y Morir.* La soledad, un problema de salud pública que aumenta el riesgo de enfermar y morir. https://elpais.com/salud-y-bienestar/2023-01-11/la-soledad-un-problema-de-salud-publica-que-aumenta-el-riesgo-de-enfermar-y-morir.html

11. *Qué Es la Depresión.* National Geographic. (2022, November 21). https://www.nationalgeographicla.com/ciencia/2022/11/que-es-la-depresion

12. U.S. Department of Health and Human Services. (2022). *Trastorno de Pánico: Cuando el Miedo Agobia. National Institute of Mental Health.* https://www.nimh.nih.gov/health/publications/espanol/trastorno-de-panico-cuando-el-miedo-agobia

13. U.S. National Library of Medicine. (n.d.). *Panic disorder.* MedlinePlus. https://medlineplus.gov/panicdisorder.html

14. https//dlerae.es/soledad

15. www.cdc.gov

16. www.cigna.com

17. www.Daystar.com

ABOUT THE AUTHOR

Pastor Marisol Santos Pagan pastored "Iglesia de Cristo Misionera, Inc., M.I." and "Iglesia El Sendero de la Cruz" for nine years in the City of Kissimmee, Florida. She holds a Bachelor's degree in Biomedical Sciences, a postgraduate degree in Medical Technology, and a Master's degree in Theology from MIZPA University.

NOTES